The International Design Library ®

American Sampler Designs

Dolores M. Andrew

When every letter with judgement
is placed
Exactly proportioned and prettily
spaced
A sampler resembles an elegant
mind
Whose passions by reason subdued
and refined.

Stemmer House

PUBLISHERS. INC.

Introduction

As computers become a more ordinary part of the lives of men and women, it is difficult to imagine a world where females were poorly educated, or even sometimes illiterate, where they were judged more for their housekeeping abilities than for their brains or professional accomplishments.

Throughout history, young girls were rarely educated, except in the functions necessary to manage a household. Their brothers had tutors or went to boarding schools where they studied mathematics, geography, history, languages. These subjects were not considered necessary for a girl to know in order to run a home. "Polite accomplishment," which meant the study of music and painting, was, however, considered important. Embroidery was also included in this category as an essential refinement, as well as a basic educational tool for girls. Embroidery in general was a "polishing" subject for young girls, and the sampler in particular was a required discipline for many of them. With it they learned the alphabet sufficiently to recognize and stitch their names, numbers enough to purchase household supplies, and some simple stitches to mark and mend their linens. The sampler taught it all.

The word "sampler" comes from the Latin "exemplum," or "example to work by." The word entered the English language from the French word "essemplaire," when French was the language of the English court. Gradually the word was shortened to its present form, "sampler."

The original purpose of samplers was as a practice cloth of stitches, without any sophistication or planning, to be used for reference and to be added to periodically. They were never intended to be works of art; they were the stitch books of the time. The earliest surviving samplers in the United States are from the seventeenth century in New England, and very few of them remain. These contain a variety of stitches, often with many complicated decorative techniques. They include closely stitched, exquisite examples of needlelace, pulled thread, whitework, cut work and stump work. Another technique, called diaper patterns, or small diagonal designs, lent itself to the small repeated elements of samplers. A woman tried out the stitches or techniques on the fabric, and kept them handy for later use.

Samplers were made in many European countries and many European museums have some in their collections. The Germans, Dutch and Swedes all brought their needlework traditions when they came to this continent, and American museums contain examples of their work also. However, since the English had settled here first, and in greater numbers, they were the major influence on the American sampler tradition. Early New England settlers brought their embroidery with them and samplers were in their workbaskets. Very little work still exists from the seventeenth century; perhaps relatively few were even stitched, owing to the priority of merely surviving in those days. More remain from the eighteenth century, when supplies became available and life became more stable in growing towns.

What are the recognizable characteristics of a sampler? Early examples were long narrow strips of fabric, usually linen, linsey-woolsey (linen warp and wool weft) or a woolen material called tammy.

The width was limited to 8" or 9", because looms were limited in size until the eighteenth century. The fabric itself was a fine count: 35 to 40 threads per inch or higher. Counted thread techniques were not always used on this fine material, but those that were resulted in exquisite, detailed work. When we remember that all of these embroideries were done without benefit of electricity, or even, sometimes, good eyesight, they are even more appreciated.

Most samplers were stitched with silk, on linen or on wool fabrics, which are the most common examples. Cotton was also sometimes used to stitch. The color of the fabric varied also. Many examples in museums are faded and delicate but probably were a natural linen color. Others seem to be pale gold or darker brown, and the linsey-woolsey material was usually a dark green or brown. Sometimes, when the fabric was a light color, the more ambitious girl stitched in the whole background, making it dark to suit herself. Of course where there are textiles, there also are bugs. What careless storage didn't ruin, the bugs usually did.

The stitches used were many and varied. Although the cross stitch is often called the "sampler stitch" because of the frequency of its appearance on schoolgirl embroideries, many other stitches were incorporated into samplers as well. The rococo stitch, or queen stitch, which means "special stitch," was also popular, especially during the eighteenth century. Other favorites were Algerian eye, long-armed cross, back, tent, chain, stem, French knots, Van Dyke, and the several stitches necessary to create the techniques mentioned above: buttonhole, satin, herringbone, eyelet, running. Darning samplers were done entirely in the running stitch, to train girls to mend household fabrics.

There seems to be no limit to the range of colors used. Early samplers, which were often rolled and stored, are in better condition, and reveal brighter colors than those which were handled a lot, and exposed to light, dust, insects and other pollutants. Of course, colors in samplers done by early American colonists were limited to those that they could obtain by dying with plants and vegetables. Colors became more varied in the eighteenth century and more widely manufactured in the mid-nineteenth. Sometimes the colors used reflected the symbolism of church seasons, but not always.

One example of an early sampler is that done by Loara Standish. She was the daughter of Miles Standish and her sampler is the oldest dated specimen existing in the United States. It has neither cross stitch nor alphabet, but does have a verse and a lot of long-armed cross in various patterns. The colors in it are green, cream, yellow, brown and buff—all possible from vegetable and plant dyes of the time. One characteristic not typical of the samplers of school girls (as Loara was estimated to be in 1643), is that it is reversible. Most schoolgirls did not accomplish this feat or even care to with their stitching.

Loara Standish's work has another characteristic which is typical of early American samplers. It is a band sampler. Stitches and patterns were done in straight, horizontal rows across the narrow width, sometimes with one stitch or pattern repeated, sometimes with different ones covering all of the material.

Another type of early sampler is called a "spot" sampler. This is identified by small stitch designs or techniques, randomly scattered across the fabric, tried out and "stored," without regard for spacing, design or even completion. In fact, many existing examples of both band and spot samplers are unfinished.

During the eighteenth and early nineteenth centuries, samplers became wider and larger, often more square, as materials became less expensive. Designs became more pictorial, using a variety of subjects, alphabets, sayings and styles. Borders were gradually introduced in the early eighteenth century, and grew wider and more important in the nineteenth, with the center motifs shrinking, taking a less important part in the design. During the Victorian period, samplers were very "busy"; every inch of the surface was covered with stitching.

Many embroidered pictures are called samplers, but really are not. They were stitched to show expertise or to commemorate an event, and while they often have a center motif and an elaborate border, they are not truly samplers. One arbitrary ruling made long ago stated that needlework signed and dated was a sampler. Otherwise, it was not. That adds a lot of confusion to an otherwise simple definition, and is misleading, considering how many unsigned and undated samplers are to be found.

Band samplers gradually changed from samplers of techniques exclusively to those including alphabets and numbers in various styles. As material became more plentiful, the spot sampler became more decorative, with more conscious effort at planning in the placement of the elements. Eventually both types of samplers merged, as rows of alphabets alternated with small designs, which were interspersed with numbers, and the whole range was repeated several times down the fabric.

Subjects used on samplers are as many and as diverse as the young girls who did them. Designs that can be identified as from the sixteenth century began as rows of stitched patterns and gradually evolved into geometric designs and shapes. These were often done in white on white. In the seventeenth century, the geometrics gradually took on a more real appearance, using color and stylized leaves, flowers and fruit. However, because of the grid nature of the even-weave fabric usually used, designs were still not completely realistic, since they were limited to stitches which went horizontally, vertically and in a 45-degree angle. One design from the early eighteenth century, the Boston Band Pattern, is a vivid example of the use of this limitation. It is a repeated geometric found on several pieces of that region.

Stylized strawberries, roses and tulips in repeat patterns were very popular during the early-to-late eighteenth century. They appeared in many forms in many works. Scholars and researchers of sampler documentation have tried in vain to develop a sequence tracing how these elements evolved, but there still seems to be no logical explanation. They existed in one form or another over several decades, possibly being copied accurately or inaccurately from other samplers or from pattern books. It is also possible that there was a religious symbolism involved, e.g., the tulip standing for the Trinity and the rose for purity.

Two other popular but obscure themes were stylized figures facing each other, called "boxers" because of their boxing stance, and the reverse "S." Both had a stylized appearance, due to the geometric design and the grid characteristic of the even-weave fabric. An altar cloth in the Dewitt-Wallace Museum in Williamsburg features a "boxer" figure and attributes such designs to Italian pattern books, which influenced English and later, American samplers.

During the eighteenth century, samplers became less notebooks of stitches by young women and more the occupation of schoolgirls. They took on the appearance that we associate with them today. Vines, berries and honeysuckle started to blossom amid the alphabets and numbers, which had previously been separated only by rows of cross stitch. Sometimes they were borders; sometimes they appeared as separate elements. Religious verses, prayers and Biblical quotations became popular after 1735.

Along with the growing interest in natural forms, some of the samplers of the eighteenth century were reminiscent of the Jacobean designs popular at the time. Large, decorative mounds, with improbable blossoms and oversize swirling leaves, make us aware that some students also knew some crewel techniques.

Mid-eighteenth century saw the introduction of Adam and Eve, the serpent and the apple trees. Adam and Eve were surrounded and often covered by large stylized leaves sprouting from the tree. The snake twined around the tree trunk. Some authorities believe that these figures were an outgrowth from the boxer figures of the previous decades. Others believe that they were merely Biblical lessons. But who is to say?

Buildings began to appear in the last third of the eighteenth century, but were not recognizable as particular locations until the 1770s. After that, many schools, homes, churches and other public buildings were dutifully depicted by schoolgirl embroiderers. Churches were often depicted with the doors left unstitched to show that the church was open.

By the end of the eighteenth century, samplers had developed distinctive regional styles, with more planning apparent, and a variety of buildings, trees, people, birds, flowers, animals and borders that accompanied the requisite alphabets and numbers. Sometimes the people and animals were larger than the buildings. Sometimes the bird did not fit on the tree. Occasionally the designs were quite beautifully executed, with good proportion and perspective, but they were the exceptions.

During the late eighteenth century, the genealogical sampler developed into another popular style. Although young girls had occasionally included names or initials of family members in their work in the earlier part of the century, whole family trees, charts or lists exist in sampler form from this time on. These must have been terribly boring to stitch, but today they are an invaluable source for anyone doing ancestor-tracing. And what a tribute to the perseverance of the stitcher!

Nineteenth-century schoolgirls stitched with more diligence, or with better teachers, and produced more "polished," designed works. They almost always contained a border of a repeated floral motif around three or all four sides. The central panel, besides having the required alphabet and numbers, could include a public building, a pious saying, a map of the United States or an attempt at one, a commemorative scene, or an imaginary one. Eagles were popular about the time of the fortieth anniversary of the Declaration of Independence.

Designs were more obviously planned, with often balanced elements and a "cleaner," less cluttered appearance. Although the relationship between the elements was still not correct, or in perspective, they were well stitched. Bowls of fruit were as big as a building. A flower, a man and a building were still equal in size. Stitching and filling the space were more important than exact relationships.

Design sources were many. As with the previous century when daughters copied from mothers or from the few existing books, during the nineteenth century they also copied designs from their teachers, and from contemporary books, engravings or paintings. Some teachers allowed no variation in their designs, and so there are many identical examples in some areas. Other teachers were more liberal and allowed some personalizing of their students' interpretations.

The designs were often drawn directly on the fabric with a pen or pencil. Sometimes they were drawn on paper which was attached under the material and stitched through it, the paper torn away when finished. Unfinished samplers show traces of both of these methods. Paint was sometimes used to enhance a design, or add subtle details. Faces were often painted. Sometimes the paint was added over the stitched areas, but more often stitches were applied over the paint.

Quotations were often included and there are hundreds of examples of them. Many are charming and fresh. Some are serious; many are morbid. They range from prayer to pious saying and Bible quotation.

A brief typical one:

> Hannah Weeks is my name,
> New England is my nation.
> Heaven is my dwelling place
> And Christ is my salvation.

Many little girls in many towns stitched this, varying it, of course, according to their town or village.

Some poems are in praise of nature; some are practice; some speak of duty to family and friends, of death and dying. Life expectancy during these times, especially for children, was short, and they were taught to accept it.

> When I am dead and in my grave
> And all my bones are rotten,
> When this you see remember me,
> That I won't be forgotten.

Some quotations are very brief, only two or three lines. Some are lengthy poems or scripture. Some speak of female education, such as it was:

Industrious ingenuity may find
Noble employment for the female mind
and
This needlework of mine was taught
Not to spend my time for naught.

Not all children stitched with the love and meekness that the existing samples would have us believe. At least one sampler exists that states that she who stitched it "hated every minute of it!" The young girl who proudly stitched her name, age and date on her childhood work often became a woman who carefully unpicked the stitches of one or both of those telltale numbers to disguise her true age in later years! While this often causes amusement to us on viewing them, it creates confusion to a serious genealogist who might find more than one person by that name in a community.

One of the most important elements of the samplers was the alphabet, since it was one of the main reasons for making them. Alphabets varied with the century, the region and the teacher. Some samplers contain only alphabets and numbers. Others have several different type faces, sometimes separated by decorative rows of abstract elements. Both upper and lower case were often included, especially if a poem or saying was used.

Spacing was not always thought out, and so imaginative devices were used. Lower case letters that normally project below the line, such as "g" or "y," were stitched sitting on the line, making some eye adjustment necessary when reading the poem. When a complete word would not fit on a line, the stitcher was creative, tucking the remaining letters above or below the line, at the beginning of the next, or wherever there was space. It could even run into the border design. We can surmise that the verse was probably stitched last, after the other parts of the design, and that the letters had to squeeze into the available area, even into the border. This too takes some concentration to decipher, but with appreciation of the stitcher's ingenuity to make it fit. Sometimes we can see the stitcher's determination and personality come through in the innovative way she solved her spacing problems.

Some letters were missing in alphabets, and others were often substituted for those we use today. J and U were missing in seventeenth and eighteenth century samplers. "Fs" was used instead of "ss."

Samplers were signed in a variety of ways. The most ostentatious included name, age and date, sometimes quite large, proudly placed in the very center of the design. Others stitched that information in a less conspicuous spot, sometimes as a subtle part of the design. Still others worked it into the repeat patterns of the alphabet bands. The more modest stitchers used only their initials, or remained anonymous, leaving out any identifying details whatsoever.

How did the children execute these very disciplined works? Where did they learn these skills? In early Colonial times, most children were taught by their mothers, using what materials were at hand. As the colonies grew and cities became larger, teachers actively competed for students from among the wealthy, as ads in contemporary newspapers attest. Those whose students could produce the most accomplished samplers were successful teachers. When the young girls came home from these schools, the embroidery was the accomplishment that was shown off. Even that much education was not free; it was considered a privilege.

Scholars who today study samplers can identify many teachers of the late eighteenth to the nineteenth century, sometimes from contemporary records, and sometimes from comparing similarity of styles or elements in students' work. For these dedicated historians, tracing creators and teachers must have many aspects of solving a mystery.

Many schools and teachers have been traced to New England in the early eighteenth century. It was a more widely settled area, more secure from Indian attack by then, and of course had more prosperous merchants, ship captains and landowners with daughters to teach. The Dame schools were an early form of education there for the young. In these gatherings in a widow's home, very simple samplers were stitched by very young children. The children, almost always girls, ranged in age from eight to fourteen years. A few examples done by boys have been found, so we know that they were taught occasionally also.

Besides the letters and stitching ability, samplers taught them obedience, patience, diligence—and "mind improving." Darning samplers was a technique taught to working-class children. Material was often cut purposely by the teacher to test the child's ability to mend it.

Although girls' schools grew in the nineteenth century, the curriculum was still centered on "accomplishments" rather than academics. One exception was the Moravians. They were a German-speaking, Protestant group that came to the colonies during the eighteenth century, settling in North Carolina. They were unusual in that they not only believed in equal education for both boys and girls, but for blacks and whites alike. They eventually founded other communities in central Pennsylvania and in Canada. The girls produced lovely needlework and samplers, but they studied some academic subjects too.

The Quakers were another religious group that offered education to girls as well as boys. The Westtown School in Pennsylvania was founded in 1799, and taught samplers along with an academic curriculum. However, girls studied samplers for two weeks out of every six, producing a series of five projects: darning, alphabets, extracts (a pious saying), geometrics, and finally, a three-dimensional globe of the world. These were about the size of a cantaloupe, stitched in silk on silk, and were sometimes all stitched, and sometimes partially watercolored. Samplers were supposed to be plain and to teach neatness, accuracy, piety and patience.

Another unusual educational opportunity in needlework was that offered in Baltimore by the Oblate Sisters of Providence, the first permanent order of African nuns. They specifically educated young black girls both in academics and in needlework, producing many fine examples of the ornate styles popular in the nineteenth century.

Although most samplers were done in New England and the Middle Atlantic areas, many have survived from the South also. It was long assumed that the climate either didn't allow for their preservation, or that young girls were sent north to study and their samplers ended up there. While these points may have some validity, there are large numbers of samplers preserved in public and private collections throughout the South, primarily in Virginia, the Carolinas, Tennessee and Kentucky.

Samplers continued to be taught in frontier and Catholic schools in the mid-nineteenth century, but gradually more academic subjects were introduced in girl's education.

Largely forgotten, the old samplers languished in family attics and on back bedroom walls for years, until the genre burst on the scene in the 1980s, as collectors discovered their value. The young girls who stitched them, and the families who kept them safe, did not dream that they would one day be contributing to knowledge of an important part of our cultural past, a past that is more removed every day as the computer culture becomes a part of our lives.

D.M.A.

Illustrations

Front Ann Barriere, Maryland 1820
Cover From the collection of the Maryland Historical Society

Title *Poem* Edwina Graham, Tennessee, 1824
Page *Border* Mary Anna King, 1834, author's collection

Back Hannah Foster, New Hampshire, 1795
Cover

Plates

1 *Top* Mary Walton, English, circa 1650
   Middle Anne Gower, Mass. 17th century
   Lower Middle Unknown, English, 17th century
   Bottom Mary Hollingworth, Mass., circa 1665
2 *Top* Elizabeth Roberts, Mass., circa 1665
   Middle Anne Austin, New England, circa 1691
   Lower Middle Mehitable Foster, New Hampshire, 1786
   Bottom Anne Austin, New England, circa 1691
3 *Top* Mary Batchelder, Mass., 1773
   Middle Mary Richardson, Mass., 1783
   Bottom Abigail Pinniger, Mass., 1730
4 *Left* Hannah Lord, Conn., 1770
   Middle Abigail Mears, 1772
   Right Thankful Davis, Mass., 1799
5 *Left* Jane Herbert, Mass., 1796
   Middle Lucy Warner, Conn., circa 1786
   Right Jemina Gorham, Rhode Island, 1790
6 *Left* Grace Welsh, 1774
   Right Ann Marsh, Philadelphia, 1730
7 *Small Butterflies* Ann Marsh, Philadelphia, 1730
   Small Flowers Hannah Batchelder, Mass., 1780
   Large Flower Anne Wing, New England, 1739
   Bottom Elizabeth Pecker, 1733
8 *Birds* Unknown, circa 1765
   Floral Mary Batchelder, Mass. 1773
   Bottom Jane Herbert, Mass. 1796
9 *Top* Sukey Makepeace, 1750
   Middle Ann Robins, 1730
   Bottom Hetty Lees, 1799
10 *Left* Hannah Taylor, Rhode Island, 1774
   Middle Anne Anthony, Mass., 1786
   Right Mary Webb, Pennsylvania, 1760
11 *Left* Eunice Lincoln, 1774
   Middle Polly Coggeshall, Conn., 1795
   Right Lydia Speakman, Philadelphia, 1785
12 *Top* Ann Peartree, Mass., 1734
   Bottom Left Unknown, 1742
   Bottom Right Detail from Dewitt-Wallace embroidery sample
13 *Top* Unknown, circa 1760
   Middle and Bottom Sarah Logan, Philadelphia, 1725
14 *Left Top* Sally Baldwin, circa 1794
   Right Top Zebiah Gore, Mass., 1791
   Bottom Anne Anthony, Mass., 1786
15 *Left Top* Eunice Bourne, Mass., circa 1745
   Right Top Eliza Cozzens, Rhode Island, 1795
   Bottom Dorothy Ashton, New England, 1764
16 *Top* Sarah Hanson, Maryland, 1783
   Middle Mary Clark, 1789
   Bottom Betsey Davis, Rhode Island, 1797
17 *Top* Sarah Hanson, Maryland, 1783
   Left Middle, Right Middle and Bottom Unknown, Mass., 1758
18 *Top* Tryphenia Collins, circa 1790
   Middle Hannah Hooper, Mary Trail, Mass., circa 1790
   Bottom Betsy Gail, Mary Bowles, Mass., circa 1790
19 *Top Left Insect* Sukey Smith, Mass., 1791
   Top Right Rebekah Jones, Philadelphia, 1750
   Middle Sukey Smith, Mass., 1791
   Lower Middle Hannah Johnson, 1768
   Bottom Mary Shillaber, Mass., 1776
20 *Upper Left* Lucy Warner, Conn., 1786

20 *Center* Loann Smith, Rhode Island, 1785
   Lower Right Ann Tingles, Maryland, 1798
   Upper Right Sally Johnson, Mass., 1799
21 *Upper Right* Anne Pope, Mass., 1796
   Upper Left Nancy Winsor, Rhode Island, 1786
   Center Right Rebecca Carters, Rhode Island, 1788
   Lower Left Sukey Smith, Mass., 1791
22 *Top* Polly Foster, New Hampshire, 1787
   Left Middle and Right Middle Naby Dane, Mass., 1789
   Center and Bottom Ann Heyl, Pennsylvania, 1789
23 *Left and Right* Sally Sanborn, New Hampshire, 1799
   Center Eliza Cozzens, Rhode Island, 1795
   Bottom Hannah Foster, New Hampshire, 1795 (example of "moustache" school, owing to leaf shape over basket)
24 Mary Clark, 1789 and Jane Humphrey, 1771
25 Mary Jones, Pennsylvania, 1795
26 *Center* Susannah Head, Pennsylvania, 1781
   Border Fanny Rimes, Pennsylvania, 1808
27 *Upper* Unknown, executed in eyelet stitch
   Center Hannah Loring, Mass., 1812
   Border Mary Jones, Pennsylvania, 1795
28 Unknown, circa 1775
29 Lucy Wyman, 1807
30 *Eighteenth century alphabet assortment*
   Upper floral Catherine Parry, South Carolina, 1739
   Center Design Henrietta Markland, Maryland, 1792
   Lower Right Elizabeth Barton, Virginia, 1798
   Lower Left Border Boston Band Pattern, Mariah Davenport, Mass., 1749
31 *Eighteenth century alphabet assortment*
   Insect Elizabeth Barton, Virginia, 1798
   Eagle Ann Tingles, Maryland, 1809
   Lower Right Philadelphia Diamond Pattern, Sarah Howell, Philadelphia, 1731
32 *Nineteenth Century Alphabet Assortment*
   Border Sophia Catherine Bier, 1810
33 *Nineteenth Century Alphabet Assortment*
   Border Maria Bake, New Jersey, 1829
34 *Left* Elizabeth Ayer, Mass., 1801
   Middle Mary Kimball, Mass., 1808
   Right Martha Jane Smith, Maryland, 1840
35 *Left* Mary Butz, Pennsylvania, 1842
   Middle Mary Cooper, New Jersey, 1814
   Right Margaret Moss, Pennsylvania, 1825
36 *Left Border* Esther Bechtell, author's collection, 1843
   Upper Sidney Jefferis, Pennsylvania, 1804
   Middle Leah Young, Pennsylvania, 1847
   Bottom Nancy Platt, 1804
37 *Upper* Margaret Moss, Pennsylvania, 1825
   Middle Susan Munson, 1824
   Bottom Sibilla Ways, Pennsylvania, 1813
   Right Border Mary Butz, Pennsylvania, 1842
38 *Top* Sally Shattuck, n.d.
   Bottom Carolyn Vaughn, 1818
39 *Top Left* Jane Norris, Maryland, n.d.
   Top Right Elizabeth Gould, Maryland, 1807
   Center and Bottom Ann Barriere, Maryland, 1820
40 *Top* Margaret Moss, Pennsylvania, 1825
   Small Peacocks Anna Eliza F..., Maryland, 1808
   Bottom Elizabeth McMachen, Maryland, 1834
41 *Top* Abigail P. Yarnall, Pennsylvania, 1817
   Left, Right, Middle Westtown School, Pennsylvania, 1837
   Lower Middle Julia Brickers, North Carolina, 1846
   Bottom Ann Barr, Pennsylvania, 1822
42 Ann Barr, Pennsylvania, 1822
   From the collection of the Lancaster Historical Society

LOCATIONS OF AMERICAN SAMPLER COLLECTIONS
partial listing

California	Fine Arts Museum of San Francisco Los Angeles County Museum of Art
Connecticut	Connecticut Historical Society, Hartford Wadsworth Atheneum, Hartford
Delaware	Delaware State Museum, Dover Historical Society of Delaware Winterthur Museum Zwannendael Museum, Lewes
District of Columbia	Museum of the D.A.R. Smithsonian Museum Textile Museum
Maine	Maine Historical Society
Maryland	Baltimore Museum of Art Maryland Historical Society St. Joseph's Academy, Emmitsburg
Massachusetts	Amherst Historical Society Concord Museum Deerfield Museum Essex Institute, Salem Historical Society of Old Newbury Marblehead Historical Society Massachusetts Historical Society Museum of Fine Arts, Boston Nantucket Historical Society Old Dartmouth Historical Society, New Bedford Old South Meeting House Pilgrim Hall, Plymouth Plymouth Antiquarian Society Sturbridge Village Worcester Art Museum
Michigan	The Exemplarary Henry Ford Museum, Dearborn Michigan Historical Society
Minnesota	Minnesota Institute of Arts
New Hampshire	New Hampshire Historical Society, Concord Old Dartmouth
New Jersey	Burlington County Historical Society Gloucester County Historical Society New Jersey State Museum, Trenton
New York	Albany Institute Brooklyn Museum Canandaigua Historical Society Cooper Hewitt Museum of Design Metropolitan Museum of Art Strong Museum, Rochester
North Carolina	Museum of the Southern Decorative Arts, Winston-Salem
Pennsylvania	Allentown Art Museum Chester County Historical Society Hershey Museum Historical Society of Pennsylvania, Philadelphia Lancaster County Historical Society, Lancaster Moravian Museum, Bethehem

	Museum of Mourning Art, Drexel Hill Philadelphia Museum of Art, Whitman Sampler Collection Westtown School, Westtown
Rhode Island	Rhode Island Historical Society Rhode Island School of Design
Texas	Houston Museum of Fine Arts
Virginia	Abby A. Rockefeller Folk Art Center, Williamsburg Colonial Williamsburg Loudon County Museum, Leesburg Valentine Museum, Richmond
Wisconsin	Milwaukee Art Museum
Canada	Museum of Civilization, Ottawa National Gallery, Ottawa

Acknowledgments

The author thanks the following institutions and individuals for providing information and help with the research for this book: Connecticut Historical Society; Wadsworth Atheneum; Museum of Fine Arts, Boston; Frank L. Horton at Museum of Early Southern Decorative Arts, Winston-Salem; Baltimore Museum of Art; Jeff Goldman at the Maryland Historical Society; Susan Messimer and Glenn Knight at the Lancaster County Historical Society; Susan Schlack at the Moravian Museum, Bethlehem, Pa.; Westtown School; Dewitt Wallace Museum; Metropolitan Museum of Art; Cooper Hewitt Museum; Zwannendael Museum, Lewes, Delaware; Joanne Harvey, Betty Ring, Martha Robinson and Carol Huber.

Elizabeth Gould, Maryland, 1807

DEDICATION

TO ELIZABETH, REBECCA AND CHRISTINE

May they always find enjoyment in doing needlework.

1

3

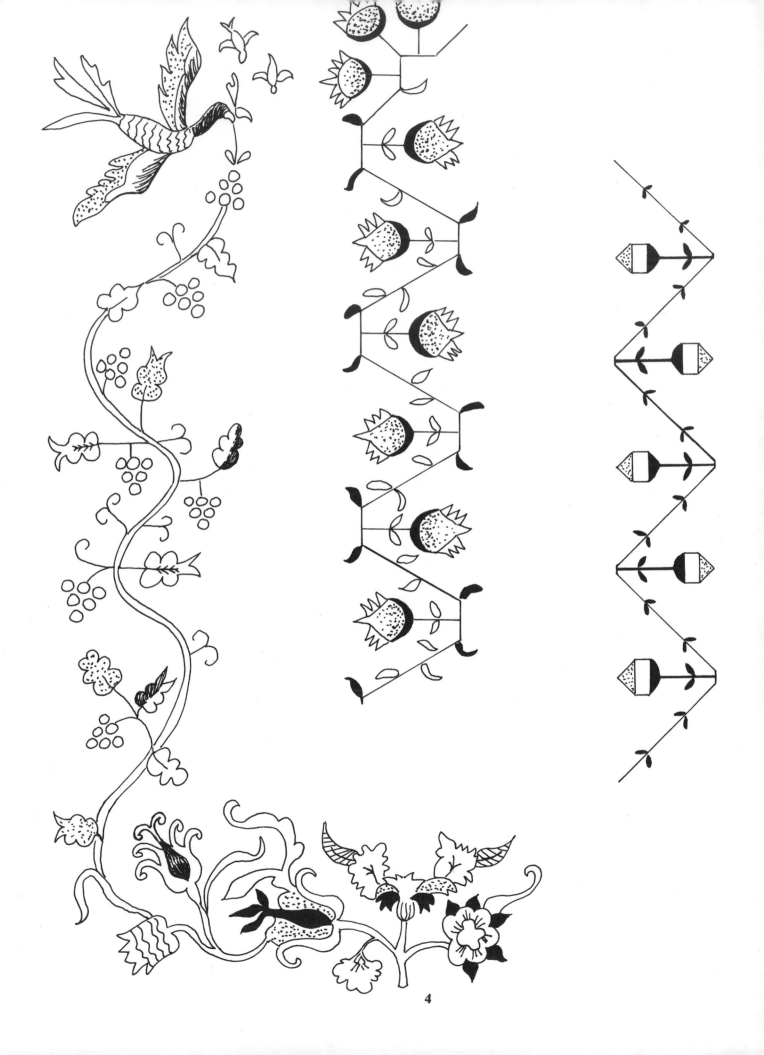

11

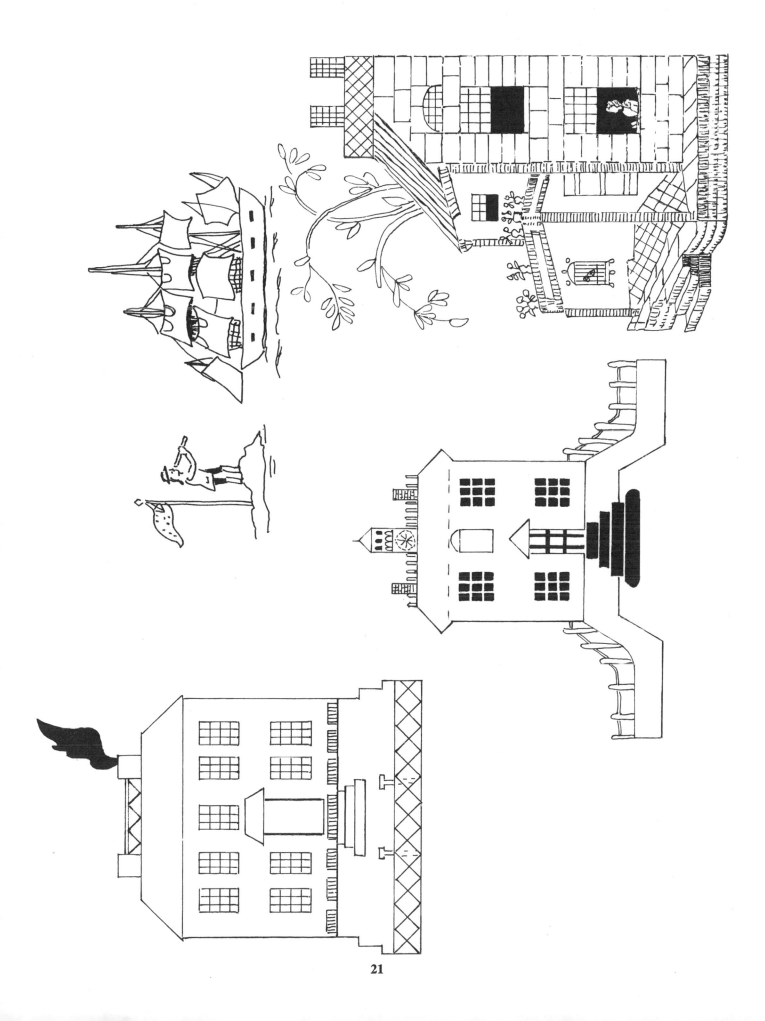

GENEALOGY

Father Mother

married

Family Record

29

A B C D E F

D E F G H

H I K L

M N O P Q R

W X Y Z

a b c d e f g h i k l m n o P q
r f s t u v w x y z & fs

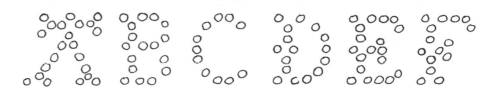

A B C D E F

G H I J K L M N

I I I O P Q R S

1 2 3 4 5

5 6 7 8 9 0

Q R S T U V

S T U V W X Y Z *

ABCDEFG

DEFGHIJK

JLKLMNBJL

NOLQRSTV

STUVWXYZ

abcdefghiklmno

lmnopqrsstvwxyz

abcdefghijklm

jklmnnopqrstu

vvwxys ffl fi

123456 456789 9

ABCDEF

GHIJKLMNOPQ

ORSTUVWX

35

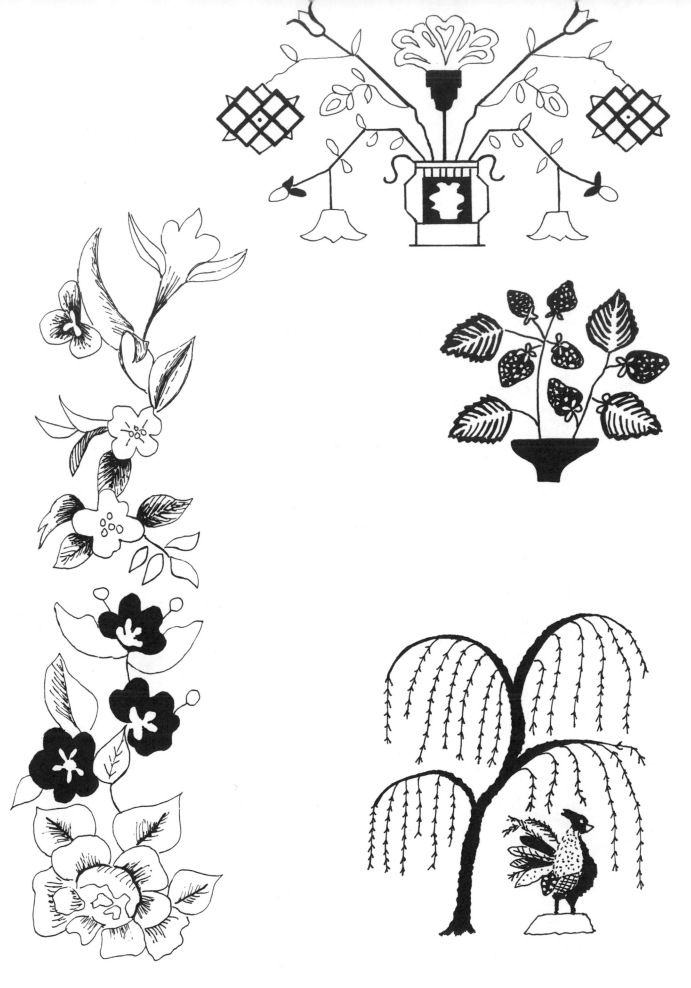

Colophon

Designed by Barbara Holdridge
Composed in Times Roman by Creative
    Computer Solutions, Baltimore,
    Maryland
Color separations by GraphTec,
    Annapolis Junction, Maryland
Printed on 80-pound Williamsburg
    Offset and bound by
    BookCrafters, Fredericksburg,
    Virginia

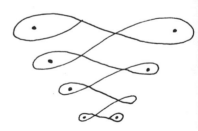